ANNULMENT

A Guide for RCIA
Candidates,
Ministers,
and
Others

KEVIN E. MCKENNA

Paulist Press
New York / Mahwah, NJ

Nihil Obstat: Rev. T. Pius Pathmarajah, J.C.L., Rev. Msgr. John J.M. Foster, J.C.D.
Censores Liborum

Imprimatur: +Most Rev. Salvatore R. Matano
Bishop of Rochester
July 24, 2015

The Scripture quotations contained herein are from the New Revised Standard Version: Catholic Edition Copyright © 1989 and 1993, by the Division of Christian Education of the National Council of the Churches of Christ in the United States of America. Used by permission. All rights reserved.

Cover and book design by Lynn Else

Library of Congress Cataloging-in-Publication Data

McKenna, Kevin E., 1950-
    Annulment : a guide for RCIA candidates, ministers, and others / Kevin E. McKenna.
       pages cm
    ISBN 978-0-8091-4957-5 (pbk.) — ISBN 978-1-58768-560-6 (e-book)
    1. Marriage—Annulment. 2. Catholic Church—Doctrines. 3. Catholic Church. Ordo initiationis Christianae adultorum. I. Title.
    BX2254.M36 2015
    262.9˙47—dc23

                                                                      2015010696

ISBN 978-0-8091-4957-5 (paperback)
ISBN 978-1-58768-560-6 (e-book)

Published by Paulist Press
997 Macarthur Boulevard
Mahwah, New Jersey 07430

www.paulistpress.com

Printed and bound in the
United States of America

CONTENTS

ACKNOWLEDGMENTS

My sincere thanks to Father Mark-David Janus, CSP, PhD, President and Publisher of Paulist Press, who first suggested this work, and to Nancy de Flon, PhD, for her much appreciated editorial assistance. I wish to express my gratitude to Bishop Salvatore Matano for his keen interest and encouragement.

I am most grateful to Rose Davis, Father Robert Kennedy, Msgr. Fred Easton, Msgr. John J. M. Foster, and Father Robert Schrader for their helpful comments, suggestions, and encouragement.

INTRODUCTION

A New Way of Welcome

Among the many changes that took place in the Roman Catholic Church after the Second Vatican Council was a new way of celebrating the welcome into the Church of new adult members. What had previously been a somewhat "private preparation" of the candidate for baptism, usually by a priest and consisting of several tutorial sessions in the rectory, now became a more public and participatory process. This involved many "stages" marked by liturgical rites, and a new teaching model in which several individuals prepare for the Sacrament of Baptism, accompanied by the Catholic community in a variety of ways through their initiation into the Church.

The Second Vatican Council's *Constitution on the Sacred Liturgy* (*SC*) had called for a renewal of the *adult catechumenate*—that is, the process of leading an unbaptized adult to faith and to the Sacrament of Baptism—and the restoration of several distinct steps with sacred rites to be celebrated in successive intervals (*SC* 64). This process is based on a tradition that goes nearly as far back as New Testament times. Another document from the Council, the *Decree on the Missionary Activity of the Church*, clarified that the purpose of the catechumenate is not just to expound doctrines but is a training period, an apprenticeship, for learning the Christian life in which catechumens (those preparing for full initiation into the Roman Catholic Church) are instructed in Christian doctrine and the practice of Christian morality (no. 14).

Additionally, the *Decree on the Pastoral Ministry of Bishops* exhorted bishops to "renew or at least adapt in a better way the instruction of adult catechumens" (no. 14). Such an initiative— the revising of the manner in which catechumens were to be fully initiated into the Church—fit well into one of the major thrusts of the Second Vatican Council: revisiting the ancient practices of the Church. Several elements of early Church practice concerning initiation were included in the revised rites and adapted to contemporary circumstances.

Another important thrust of this new form of welcome was the opportunity for those already initiated into the faith—that is, those who were already Catholic—to be renewed as they reflected with the catechumens on the paschal mystery and the need for frequent conversion of heart to the gospel message.

A PERSONAL JOURNEY IN COMMUNITY

Many parish communities enthusiastically adopted this model of initiation, welcoming its potential for helping the entire parish in its responsibility of "searching out those who are searching" and walking with them in their journey to a home in the Catholic Church. Those charged with overseeing what became known as the Rite of Christian Initiation of Adults (RCIA) marveled at the faith stories that were shared by the many who responded to the invitation to explore in depth the Catholic Church and to consider that it might hold the answers to their questions about God and faith. While no two journeys were ever the same, participants were fascinated by the similar conclusions they had reached. Their communal reflections revealed an appreciation of God's mysterious ways, a common sense that the Catholic Church was where they belonged. The process has also offered an opportunity for those already initiated to reflect prayerfully and thank God for their own unique and personal journeys of faith.

With this revised rite or RCIA, the Church hoped to accomplish an appropriate welcome into the Catholic household: "Adults, who after hearing the mystery of Christ proclaimed, consciously and freely seek the living God and enter the way of faith and conversion as the Holy Spirit opens their hearts" (RCIA 1).

THE SPIRITUAL LIFE AS JOURNEY

The restored RCIA emphasizes the spiritual life and search for God as a "journey": "The rite of initiation is suited to a spiritual journey of adults that varies according to the many forms of God's grace, the free cooperation of the individuals, the action of the Church and the circumstances of time and place" (RCIA 5). Let us reflect on these words in detail.

"Many forms of God's grace"

The Bible is full of stories about the response of man and woman to the call of God's grace. Sometimes in a very obvious way, but sometimes in a quite subtle way, God's invitation to an individual for a relationship or a deeper relationship or a special task comes mysteriously. The Book of Exodus tells us of a remarkable revelation of God to Moses from Horeb, "the mountain of God" (Exod 3). First, God reveals himself to Moses in a burning bush that is not consumed, though it is on fire, which piques the curiosity of Moses to explore this mysterious happening. After gaining Moses' attention, God speaks to him from the Holy Ground of the mountain on which he reveals himself to Moses and shares his concern about the plight of the Israelites and their slavery in the hands of the Egyptians. Most disconcerting to Moses in this revelation was that God's plan included Moses as the one who was to lead the people from slavery out of Egypt. A conversation takes place between God and Moses in which God assures him that he will be with him in this effort: "I will be with you" (Exod 3:12).

The Scriptures recount many similar experiences in which God calls and individuals respond—although oftentimes reluctantly!

God continues to call, invite, cajole, and argue with people. In the Acts of the Apostles, we read about how the young Pharisee Saul, who persecuted the early Christians but was later known as St. Paul, encountered Jesus on the road to Damascus as he travelled to arrest the Lord's disciples. Paul powerfully experienced the call to a conversion of heart and a new life completely committed to the gospel. It was clear to Paul that this all transpired through the grace of God, who called him to a new journey. "But when God, who had set me apart before I was born and called me through his grace, was pleased to reveal his Son to me, so that I might proclaim him among the Gentiles" (Gal 1:15–16a).

"The free cooperation of the individuals"

The Scriptures relate how God communicated his plan to various individuals and awaited a response. Mary received the incredible news that she was to bear a son and "of his kingdom there will be no end" (Luke 1:33). After presenting some preliminary questions about such a call ("How can this be, since I am a virgin?" [1:34]), she ultimately responded to God, "Let it be with me according to your word" (1:38). We too can have questions when we sense we are being called to a conversion, a change of heart, or a new direction. Questions perhaps fill our minds. But God always waits for our free assent to his invitation. It takes a "leap of faith" to trust that God is leading us in a direction that will be ultimately life-giving.

"The action of the Church"

The Second Vatican Council describes the Church as a "pilgrim" Church, on the move, proclaiming the Kingdom of God with the help and guidance of the Holy Spirit. The Vatican II *Dogmatic Constitution on the Church (LG)* refers to the church as the universal sacrament of salvation, with Jesus "continually active in the world, leading [people] to the Church, and through her joining them more closely to Himself and making them partakers of His glorious life by nourishing them with His own body and blood" (*LG* 48). In *The Joy of the Gospel (EG)*, a document known as an "Apostolic Exhortation," Pope Francis has vigorously reminded members of the Church of their responsibility to bring about the Kingdom by their own initiatives and fidelity to living the Gospel message. The pope speaks of many who today are "quietly seeking God, led by a yearning to see his face" (*EG* 14). Christians have the responsibility to appear as "people who wish to share their joy, who point to a horizon of beauty and who invite others to a delicious banquet. It is not by proselytizing that the Church grows, but by attraction" (*EG* 14).

"The circumstances of time and place"

Sometimes God can enter our lives at what feels like the most inconvenient of times. Perhaps while we struggle with care for a loved one in hospice, navigate a distressed daughter going through a messy divorce, or prepare for another apparently fruitless job interview—a nagging voice invites or calls us to even deeper questions about the issues or challenges we face. Wouldn't another time be better, we might think, perhaps while I am on vacation with more leisure time? Or when I am home instead of at the hospital, and not so concerned about the care my spouse is receiving? But very often we are not the determiners of how and when God makes a connection. The spiritual journey is winding and often confusing. But when God says "the time is now," we must respond. It may not be a convenient time when we realize that God is extending an invitation for us to consider a "new way"—but we should listen!

By stressing the individual journey motif, the RCIA process acknowledges and appreciates the uniqueness of each person's search for God and the manner and time in which the individual responds. Some enter the RCIA after a long search during which they have explored a variety of faith communities or religious experiences before deciding they want to call the Catholic Church "home." Others have been adrift with no religious affiliation when quite suddenly, or even dramatically, an event or circumstance transpires to lead them to search for the meaning in their experience. Sometimes, perhaps with the help of a relative, friend, or neighbor, they find that God seems to be revealing a profound answer to them that leads to the Catholic Church. Others decide to make the leap through a marriage partner who is already a member of the Church, and through them, hear and observe Catholic practices and beliefs.

The journeys and reasons for coming to the Church are as many and varied as the thousands of people who have entered the RCIA. And so the rites have been designed with a certain flexibility so that they may honor the individuality of each journey and respect the personal history that has intersected with God's presence and design. Especially pertinent is the length of time one might need in completing the journey through the preparation and the rites and culminating in the baptism itself. For some, given their personal history and a certain exposure to the teachings of the Catholic Church, their readiness to enter the Church is exceptional; others might find themselves in need of a prolonged time of questioning and discerning before they are ready to accept baptism. There are still others who fall somewhere in between. Parish leadership performs an invaluable service in "walking the walk" with the inquirers, giving them space but also conversations, listening carefully to the details of their journey and helping them to decide how long a time might be appropriate.

THE SEEKER'S MARITAL STATUS

The marital status of the individual who may be seeking baptism in the Catholic Church is an important factor that affects the length of preparation time that may be needed. Sometimes those who inquire about Christian initiation are in what are called "irregular marriages," that is, marriages that are not considered to be valid according to the Catholic Church's understanding of what a marriage should be. Perhaps the inquirer has been previously married and is now in a civil union, or may be civilly married to someone who has been previously married. Because the individual cannot fully participate in the sacraments while in what is an invalid union according to church law, it is necessary that a person in an irregular marriage be free to marry prior to the celebration of the Sacraments of Initiation.

In this book I will explain the present church (or "canon") law in regards to marriage in the hope, first, that it helps those who are seeking to be baptized into the Roman Catholic Church or to be received into full communion with the Church but who are presently in what the Church considers to be an irregular union, and second, that it will also be of use to their sponsors and others who accompany them on their journey toward Christian initiation. I will briefly outline the theology of marriage as understood in the Catholic Church, provide an overview of the role of law in the Church, and then explain the various procedures that are utilized to "regularize" marriages, especially the "declaration of nullity" or annulment, which is a statement that, *according to Church law*, a given marriage was not valid (and therefore not binding) at the time a couple exchanged their marriage vows. I will discuss when a declaration of nullity is needed, what it involves, the steps of the process, and the anticipated outcome.

Furthermore, I will offer some practical guidance—including a summary of the common grounds used in the annulment proceeding—and will review some suggestions about submitting a case. Some people who have sought a declaration of nullity have not only found the results of the process—a decree of nullity and the freedom to marry in the Church—to be a blessing, but have also found the process itself to be healing and helpful as they sorted out issues connected to a prior union and its related problems.

Pope Francis has issued two decrees—*The Gentle Judge, The Lord Jesus* and *The Meek and Merciful Jesus*—that have streamlined the annulment process to make it less cumbersome and expensive. He has also introduced some changes in the legal structures with the aim that "the heart of the faithful awaiting clarification [of their marital status] is not long oppressed by the darkness of doubt." He has asked that the process now be offered free of charge and has created an expedited process for certain cases in which the evidence of nullity is abundant and both parties believe the marriage is invalid.

This book is intended to provide guidance for the inquirer who seeks to learn about the Catholic Church's understanding about marriage and what steps may be necessary in a marriage that the Church cannot recognize due to some defect or impediment. A little book like this cannot, however, replace a conversation with a priest or knowledgeable pastoral leader who can review the individual's journey, especially the marriage, and offer helpful guidance. If you are in the process of inquiring about initiation into the Catholic sacraments or are considering beginning the process, I encourage you to contact the parish priest or knowledgeable staff member at your local parish in order to begin such a conversation.

INTRODUCTION HIGHLIGHTS

- The Second Vatican Council introduced a new way of welcoming new adult members to the Church.
- There was a return to the rituals of the early Church.
- Catholics have been invited to renewal in their own faith as they journey with the inquirers.
- Every person's search for God and a Community of Believers is unique.
- The Scriptures are filled with great figures, like Paul, who struggled to know God's call.
- In choosing to join the Roman Catholic Church, it is important to review one's marital status and the steps that may be needed prior to baptism or coming to full communion with the Church.
- Some inquirers may need to apply for a declaration of nullity, using the process provided in the Church's legal system—contained in the Code of Canon Law.
- Parish priests and parish staff members are available to assist inquirers in this process.

1

THE ROLE OF LAW IN THE CHURCH TODAY

The Roman Catholic Church, similar to other societies, organizations, and cultures, has a legal system. As with other organizations, Church law serves as a unifying instrument to help its members honor and respect the common good and the other individuals who make up the society. We refer to the law of the Church as "canon law."

WHAT IS CANON LAW?

The term *canon* derives from a Greek word referring to a rule or a straight rod and began to refer to any kind of legal norm. It is understood as a rule or statement of law. A code is a collection of these rules or laws. The first Code of Canon Law was issued for the Latin Church in 1917, and Pope John Paul II issued an updated and revised Code of Canon Law in 1983. The first codification in 1917 was an effort to assist the Church by ensuring that the same laws were operative for the entire Church. The majority of the canons are "Church-made," that is, formulated by those in the Church with the authority to make norms that affect our internal discipline, creating right order so that we might all "walk together" in our journey of faith without trampling on one another's rights.

The second codification, in 1983, also attempted to provide a common tool for helping us to walk together. It incorporated many of the insights of the Second Vatican Council (1962–65) in its legislation so that the universal law of the Church could be updated for the new circumstances and the times in which the Church found itself.

Canon law can be seen as a vehicle for serving and protecting those parts of the institutional Church that are needed to provide a certain stability in living out the Christian commitment. Also to be understood, within the context of the Church and its laws, is that the ability of mature people to make responsible decisions must be respected as they respond to the call of Christ to live the Christian message.

Since the Second Vatican Council, the Church has emphasized "communion"—communion with Christ, communion among companions on the journey of the kingdom, and communion among the local churches. This concept of communion calls for structure, within which the unique individuality, talent, and gifts of each member of the Church can be respected, esteemed, and creatively developed for service. But this can only happen when the rights of individuals within the community are respected and protected.

There has been an increasing awareness, on the part of canonists, of canon law's relationship to theology. The manner in which the faith of the Church is studied and articulated assists the community in developing its values and vision. The Catholic Church has a long and rich tradition of reflecting theologically on the major tenets of the faith—for example, the resurrection of Jesus Christ, the divine and human natures of Jesus, the trinitarian nature of God (Three Persons in one God)—in an effort to make them more understandable, especially as the times change. What might have been easily understood within a predominantly Christian culture may need an explanation in more contemporary terminology or examples, due to society's changing vocabularies and technological advancements. While maintaining adherence to the truths of the faith as they have been formally proclaimed by the Church, theologians have also attempted to explain them with images, language, and categories that might be more compatible with modern times.

The role of theology in relation to canon law is to assist the community in developing its values based on the truths of the faith. Canon law assists the community by providing norms for action that help appropriate the values that are meant to serve best the community in some practical way. For example, theologians have attempted for centuries to develop an understanding of the Sacrament of Marriage using Scripture and theological reflection. These studies have underlined the importance of the unity (marriage is the union of one husband and wife) and indissolubility (the unbreakable bond of marriage). Canon law has constructed norms for action that protect these values.

Perhaps the most dramatic development in the 1983 Code of Canon Law was the recognition of an array of rights that have been formalized and legislated. For example, all the Christian faithful have the right (in accord with their "knowledge, competence and preeminence") to make known their needs and desires to their pastors and to manifest their opinion on matters that pertain to the good of the Church (cann. 212, sec. 3). Catholics also have the right to let their pastors know of their spiritual needs (cann. 213), to enjoy academic freedom while observing "due respect for the magisterium" (teaching authority of the Church, cann. 218), and to receive a fair hearing and protection from improperly imposed sanctions (cann. 221).

The Church has continued to express and clearly specify the claims of human dignity. In recent times, this has given rise to what may be called a Roman Catholic human rights tradition. The teaching of various popes in the last three centuries has contributed to a developing canonical awareness of the rights of the individual that the legal apparatus of the Church must foster and protect. Some of these human rights have been specifically included in the Code of Canon Law, including the right to privacy and to protection of one's good name (cann. 220). It seems apparent that the canonist is now required to make sure that the "work of justice" becomes part of his or her ministry. This affects many of the issues that emerge nowadays in the typical diocese, such as employment and discrimination.

MARRIAGE AND CANON LAW

The place that has become very closely identified with the practice of canon law is the marriage tribunal of the local diocese. This tribunal serves primarily as a marriage court for Catholics (and others) who seek a declaration of nullity, or annulment. (Although the term *annulment* is often used in the text due to its familiarity, the proper term is *declaration of nullity*. The Church does not annul marriages; rather the Church declares a marriage to be invalid.) Like all of the sacraments, the Sacrament of Matrimony has seen a long development in theology and law. Although the process for obtaining a declaration of nullity is a legal one that follows carefully delineated steps and norms, many canonists who are involved in tribunal work see themselves as being involved in a ministry of service to God's people. Many who seek an annulment come to the tribunal with serious pastoral needs, perhaps the result of the personal issues related to the divorce. In his "Apostolic Exhortation on the Family" (*Familiaris Consortio*), St. John Paul II reminded pastoral ministers of their important responsibility to assist members of the faith community who have suffered the tragedy of a failed marriage: "I earnestly call upon pastors and the whole community of the faithful to help the divorced and with solicitous care to make sure that they do not consider themselves as separated from the Church, for as baptized persons, they can and indeed must share in her life."[1]

The Roman Catholic Church has continued to teach the sacredness and sacramentality of marriage within the context of its marriage law. Matrimony is one of the seven sacraments of the Church, "perceptible signs (words and actions) accessible to our human nature. By the action of Christ and the power of the Holy Spirit, they make present efficaciously the grace that they signify" (*Catechism of the Catholic Church* 1084). The Church's Code of Canon Law describes matrimony as a covenant "by which a man and a woman establish between themselves a partnership of the

---

1. Pope John Paul II, "Apostolic Exhortation on the Family," *Origins* 11 (1981): 437–68, at 465.

whole of life…by its nature ordered toward the good of the spouses and the procreation and the education of offspring; this covenant between baptized persons has been raised by Christ the Lord to the dignity of a sacrament" (cann. 1055, sec. 1). The sacraments can be seen as an encounter between the Lord and the believers within the community. Church law attempts to ensure the integrity of these encounters. The Sacrament of Marriage is a unique interpersonal relationship between baptized consenting parties who, in the presence of the church's minister, grant and accept certain mutual rights and responsibilities. Canon law attempts to safeguard the integrity of the marriage and the consent that was given, not only for the benefit of the parties themselves, but for the benefit of the larger Christian community and the larger society as well. This area of Church law includes establishing norms for marriage preparation, determining certain impediments (legal and doctrinal obstacles to the marriage actually taking effect), specifying the manner of consent, and if necessary and sadly, adjudicating cases of marriage nullity, following precise norms and procedures.

As an instrument for discernment in this regard, the Church has for centuries utilized, with some modifications and developments, a legal institute known as the *tribunal*, or Church court. In the tribunal, Church personnel trained in the law of the Church review applications submitted for a review of the possible declaration of an invalid marriage. Note that the tribunal cannot "nullify" a marriage. The role of the tribunal and Church law and the processes provided is to *examine* the marital union in question, review the material that is submitted, take testimony from witnesses, and come to a determination, with moral certitude, that the union was indeed an invalid marriage.

The process can take several months or even a year or more. There are many variables that influence the length of time it takes for a decision to be made: cooperation of the petitioner (person requesting a review of a marriage) and respondent (former spouse of the petitioner), availability of documents required, cooperation of witnesses that will be contacted, and so forth. There is never a guarantee of the outcome after the review of the case. A presumption of canon law is that all marriages brought to the tribunal concerning possible invalidity are to be regarded as valid unless and until the contrary is proven (cann. 1060). If there is the intention of entering a new marriage after the obtaining of the annulment, no date for a Church wedding can be made until the decree for the declaration of nullity has been obtained (cann. 1060). An annulment is a declaration by the Church tribunal that, contrary to what appears to be a valid marriage, a certain relationship does not fulfill the full legal and doctrinal requisites to be recognized as such by the church community.

A basic frame of reference for ecclesiastical courts is the Church's teaching on the *indissolubility* of marriage, which is understood to mean that a marriage between two baptized Christians and consummated may not be dissolved by any human authority.

MARRIAGE AS COVENANT

The Second Vatican Council was helpful in articulating and emphasizing the nature of marriage as a *covenant*, a biblical term prominent in the Hebrew Scriptures (Old Testament). God entered into a relationship of love and commitment with his chosen people, establishing reciprocal obligations that the love might flourish. Personal commitment and a relationship were primary elements. Rather than a rigid contract, God desired a covenant that would be enhanced in the heart of Israel as it became ever more aware and grateful for God's never-ending faithfulness and love for his people. God often had to renew the covenant since Israel often apostatized and rejected their part of the covenant with God:

> The days are surely coming, says the LORD, when I will make a new covenant with the house of Israel and the house of Judah. It will not be like the covenant that I made with their ancestors when I took them by the hand to bring them out of the land of Egypt—a covenant that they broke, though I was their husband, says the LORD. But this is the covenant that I will make with the house of Israel after those days, says the LORD: I will put my law within them, and I will write it on their hearts; and I will be their God, and they shall be my people. (Jer 31:31–34)

St. Paul in his Letter to the Ephesians (5:25–33) was to use the concept of a covenant in his understanding of marriage:

> Husbands, love your wives, just as Christ loved the church and gave himself up for her, in order to make her holy by cleansing her with the washing of water by the word, so as to present the church to himself in splendor, without a spot or wrinkle or anything of the kind—yes, so that she may be holy and without blemish. In the same way, husbands should love their wives as they do their own bodies. He who loves his wife loves himself. For no one ever hates his own body, but he nourishes and tenderly cares for it, just

as Christ does for the church, because we are members of his body. "For this reason a man will leave his father and mother and be joined to his wife, and the two will become one flesh." This is a great mystery, and I am applying it to Christ and the church. Each of you, however, should love his wife as himself, and a wife should respect her husband.

The Second Vatican Council, in its *Pastoral Constitution on the Church in the Modern World* (*GS*), teaches the importance of conjugal love in the relationship of the spouses:

> Thus a man and a woman, who by the marriage covenant of conjugal love "are no longer two, but one flesh" (Matt 19:6), render mutual help and service to each other through an intimate union of their actions. Through this union they experience the meaning of their oneness and attain to it with growing perfection day by day. As a mutual gift of two persons, this intimate union, as well as the good of the children, imposes total fidelity on the spouses and argues for an unbreakable oneness between them. (no. 48)

The love that is such an important part of the marital relationship is a reflection of the love Jesus has for the Church: "Christ the Lord abundantly blessed this many-faceted love, welling up as it does from the fountain of divine love and structured as it is on the model of His union with the Church" (*GS* 48).

In the coming chapters, I will attempt to assist you with helpful information about the Church's understanding of marriage, an examination of marital relationships that may be considered "invalid," and for those in need of a declaration of nullity, some useful background information about the annulment process in the Catholic Church.

CHAPTER HIGHLIGHTS

- The Roman Catholic Church has its own unique legal system, called "canon law."
- The legal system in the Church helps us to "walk together" and respect each person's rights.
- The most recent codification of Roman Catholic Church Law took place in 1983 and incorporated many of the changes of the Second Vatican Council in its formulation.
- An important contribution of the 1983 Code of Canon Law was its emphasis on the rights of its members.
- The Catholic Church has marriage courts, or "tribunals" that examine the possible invalidity of marriages.
- Sometimes a person asks a marriage tribunal to examine the possibility of the invalidity of a marriage, using a legal procedure that stresses respect for the rights of both parties involved.
- There are many variables that affect the outcome and the time it takes to establish the possible invalidity of a marriage.
- It is the belief of the Catholic Church that a marriage once truly established between two baptized Christians and consummated cannot be dissolved by any human power.

2

What Is a Declaration of Nullity (Annulment)?

Frequently, a person who seeks initiation into the Roman Catholic Church is in a marriage that cannot be recognized in Church law, or what the church calls an "irregular marriage." The person may have been previously married, was divorced, and is now in a civil union; or perhaps the person is married to someone who has been previously married. In such cases, the person would not be able to participate in the sacraments while in an invalid union and would need to establish their freedom to marry before celebrating the Sacraments of Initiation.

For this reason, it is important that those responsible for the RCIA process review the candidate's journey and thoroughly explore the issues related to what may be an irregular marriage. While the type and complexity of the variety of situations and cases make it difficult for me to address every possible marriage scenario in this short book, I will provide general guidance and some background about the process that is normally followed when a person seeking initiation into the Roman Catholic Church needs a declaration of nullity. It is therefore important that, if you believe you may be in such a situation, you consult the pastor or other member of the pastoral team for guidance when issues related to the possible need of a declaration of nullity surface. You should also be aware that, although tribunals throughout the universal Church follow the same procedures for examining possible marriage nullity, tribunals vary greatly in the amount of personnel they have available, and this can affect the amount of time it might take to process a petition. The local diocesan tribunal should always be consulted when such issues and questions arise.

What process does the tribunal follow in evaluating an application for annulment?

The following is a brief overview of the process. Please consult the area tribunal for any local adaptations:

1. A *libellus* (petition seeking an examination of a case to determine the possible invalidity of a marriage) is presented to the tribunal (cann. 1502).
2. The judge either accepts or rejects the petition (*libellus*) that has been submitted after examining it to determine whether or not the local court has competence (jurisdiction) to examine the case (cann. 1505).
3. The other party to the case, the respondent (former spouse), is cited and invited to participate, should they so desire (cann. 1507, 1508).
4. After consulting both parties in the case, the judge *formulates the doubt*, that is, determines the issues and makes a preliminary decision as to whether there will be sufficient proofs available to make a judgment concerning the possible invalidity of the marriage. At this "joinder of

issues," the grounds are selected that will be the basis for the determination about the invalidity of the marriage (cann. 1513–16).

5. The tribunal utilizes documents and witnesses to help the judge(s) reach a conclusion about the validity of the marriage (cann. 1526–29, 1547–73).

6. As part of the process, the parties to the case and their advocates will be invited to review the acts (proceedings) of the case at the tribunal. If there is a legitimate concern by the judge that there could be some serious danger to one of the parties that might result from the inspection of the acts, the judge could decide that a certain act (for example, testimony) of the case is not to be shared with the parties. The judge must be careful, however, not to jeopardize the right of defense (cann. 1598).

7. When the parties declare that there is nothing that they wish to add to the case, the judge will determine an appropriate time limit for the advocates and the defender of the bond to make final pleadings for the case and will also establish that the time for proposing further proofs has expired. The judge then declares that the case has been sufficiently instructed and ready for the final steps (cann. 1599).

8. The *defender of the bond*—an officer of the tribunal— now intervenes to propose an argument, after carefully reviewing the case, in favor of the marriage bond (cann. 1432–1602).

9. The judge in the case (or sometimes a three-judge panel) makes a decision regarding the validity of the marriage (cann. 1607–10).

10. The sentence, which includes the decision of the case and the rationale for the decision, is published, that is, it is issued to the parties. Along with the sentence is included the means and procedure of appealing the sentence if either party so desires (cann. 1611–18).

Who will be evaluating the application?

Upon submitting a case to the marriage tribunal of a diocese, the petitioner will receive correspondence from the court advising as to progress, perhaps requesting further information, clarifications, or other related matters. This correspondence will sometimes make mention of various officers of the tribunal:

- The *judge* is a person appointed by the bishop of the diocese to review cases submitted to the tribunal for a determination of the invalidity of a marriage in question, after a serious and thorough study of the materials submitted for review. A layperson may serve in this capacity, providing they have obtained the proper credentialing (degree in canon law), and must serve with a collegiate tribunal, in other words, with at least two other judges who are clerics (cann. 1446–57).
- The *defender of the bond* is appointed by the bishop to serve in the tribunal by defending the bond of marriage. This person (cleric or lay) must have a doctorate (or at least a licentiate degree) in canon law. In every case, a defender of the bond must review the acts of the case and uphold for the court the validity of the marriage bond of the case that has been submitted.
- The *assessor* is a member of the marriage tribunal who

works as a consultant and assistant to the judge as needed.

- The *ponens* refers to the judge who writes the sentence for the case (cann. 1429) in a collegiate tribunal, that is, when at least three judges are used.
- The *auditor* is a member of the tribunal staff who assembles the proofs that will be needed for the case, according to the mandate of the judge (cann. 1428).
- A *notary* officially signs and thereby authenticates the acts of the case (cann. 1437).
- The *advocate* is an individual, properly delegated, who protects the rights of one of the parties during the annulment process and provides the parties legal advice.

How does the annulment process begin?

The annulment process normally begins with an appointment with a priest, deacon, or parish staff member. This pastoral person will be familiar with the local diocesan procedures and can assist in the preparation of the case. Some tribunals request that the applicant complete a comprehensive questionnaire, so that the tribunal may begin the process with a solid overview of the marriage in question as well as the individuals who entered into the marriage. Other tribunals use a brief application form, augmented by an extensive interview between a representative of the tribunal and the applicant. Some dioceses ask parish staff members to act as case "sponsors," to assist the petitioner by ensuring that the application is complete and following up with him or her, and assisting both the applicant and the tribunal as the case proceeds. Once again, I want to stress that the local parish will be the best resource to begin the process for obtaining a declaration of nullity.

The annulment process is a religious process with no civil law effects, such as custody of children, which need to be settled before the tribunal process may begin. Therefore a civil divorce is needed before the Church annulment process can begin, to show there is no hope for reconciliation between the parties.

In the next chapter, I will review some of the grounds that are used by tribunals in establishing the validity or invalidity of the marriage in question.

CHAPTER HIGHLIGHTS

- The Church utilizes a legal procedure for examining the possible invalidity of a marriage.
- The procedure involves establishing the grounds (the basis in Church law) by which the marriage in question will be examined.
- The former spouse and witnesses, parties who knew either or both spouses, will be invited to participate in the process.
- The person who initiates the process ("petitioner") has the opportunity, along with the former spouse ("respondent"), to review the material that has been assembled for the case.
- Several tribunal officials will be involved in the case, each with a particular role as given by the law of the Church.

- Normally, the person desiring a declaration of nullity is assisted by the parish priest, deacon, or knowledgeable parish staff members in the preparation of the case and will be available for consultation as the case progresses.

3

WHAT ARE THE POSSIBLE GROUNDS FOR NULLITY?

In this chapter, I will briefly outline some of the possible grounds on which a marriage may be considered invalid. I will also outline circumstances in which one may petition for the dissolution of a marriage. Some marriages may be considered invalid for the following reasons:

1. The presence of an impediment
2. A defect of canonical form
3. A defect of consent

1. The presence of an impediment

An *impediment* is something that canon law regards as an "obstacle" that prevents a valid and licit sacrament from being celebrated. When an impediment exists, it prevents a person from celebrating marriage validly. Sometimes an impediment can be proven publicly; this is referred to as a "public impediment." Otherwise, it is referred to as an "occult [hidden] impediment." Some impediments have been determined by the Church and these impediments can be dispensed (*dispensation* is relaxation of a Church law by someone who is authorized). Other impediments are from divine law, revealed by God, and therefore cannot be dispensed. Some ecclesiastical (church) impediments are reserved for dispensation to the Holy See; however, many impediments can be dispensed by the local bishop.

The bishop can dispense from every ecclesiastical impediment for those members of his diocese who are in danger of death wherever they might be as well as from the canonical form of marriage (see following), with the exception of the impediment of the sacred order of the presbyterate—he cannot release a priest from his obligation of celibacy even when the priest might be in danger of death. When the bishop cannot be reached to grant the needed dispensation, the pastor, priest, deacon, or properly delegated minister may also dispense from the same impediments. Sometimes it may happen that a pastoral minister, when about to celebrate a marriage, has inadvertently omitted obtaining a needed dispensation from an impediment. In such circumstances, when the impediments are occult (not publicly known), the minister may dispense the impediments with the exception of Sacred Orders, crime, and consanguinity in the direct line or in the second degree of the collateral line (see following).

What specific impediments may invalidate a marriage?

- *Age* (cann. 1083)
  A man under sixteen years of age or a woman who is under fourteen years of age cannot validly enter into marriage.
- *Impotence* (cann. 1084)
  Antecedent (before the marriage) and perpetual (ongoing

and continuing) inability to have sexual intercourse, whether it be in the man or in the woman, and whether absolute (always incapable) or relative (with this particular partner), invalidates a marriage. If the presence of the impediment is doubtful, the marriage is not to be impeded or to be declared null while the doubt persists.

- *Prior Bond* (cann. 1085)

  A person who is bound by a prior valid marriage, even if the marriage has not been consummated, contracts marriage invalidly. The person cannot contract a valid marriage until the invalidity of the marriage has been established with certainty.

- *Disparity of Cult* (cann. 1086–1125, 1126)

  Cult here refers to whether the persons involved are baptized Catholics (or who have been received into the Church) or unbaptized persons. Marriage between a baptized Catholic (or one who has been received into the Catholic Church) and a person who is not baptized is considered invalid. Before the impediment can be dispensed, however, certain conditions must be fulfilled:

  1. The Catholic party must declare that he or she is ready to remove any dangers of falling away from the faith and make a sincere promise to do all in his or her power to have all children born of the union baptized and raised in the Catholic Church.
  2. The other party must be informed at an appropriate time concerning this declaration and promise and must be fully aware of the obligations accepted by the Catholic party.

3. Both of the parties are to be instructed about the essential ends and properties of marriage.

If it was presumed at the time of the marriage that one party was baptized or even if it was doubted, the marriage is presumed to be valid until it is proven that one party was not baptized and the other party was baptized. A Catholic who wishes to marry a baptized member of another faith tradition must make the same promises as those listed above. In this latter case, however, it is *permission* that is sought from the diocesan bishop and not a *dispensation from an impediment*. Without the proper dispensation from an impediment, the marriage is considered invalid. Without permission, it is considered valid but illicit, that is, it was unlawful since a proper procedure was not followed.

- *Sacred Orders* (cann. 1087)

  Those persons who have received sacred orders (that is, ordination to the diaconate, priesthood, or episcopate) attempt marriage invalidly.

- *Vows of Chastity* (cann. 1088)

  A person who has publicly professed perpetual vows in a religious institute (that is, made vows as a member of a religious community) and who attempts marriage does so invalidly.

- *Abduction* (cann. 1089)

  A marriage that is attempted between a man and a woman who has been abducted, or at least detained, is invalid until the woman freely gives her consent after being released.

- *Crime* (cann. 1090)

  A marriage that is attempted by an individual who, for the purpose of marriage with a certain person, brings about the death of that person's present spouse or one's own spouse is invalid. A couple also invalidly attempts marriage if they bring about the death of their spouses through mutual physical or moral cooperation.

- *Consanguinity* (relationship by blood, cann 1091)

  A marriage is invalid between a person and all descendants and ancestors in the *direct line* (parent, grandparent, son, grandson, and so forth), whether the relationship is legitimate (that is, through marriage) or natural. A marriage is also invalid in the *collateral* line (for example, siblings, cousins, and so on,) up to and including the *fourth degree* (first cousins). Marriage is never permitted if there is a doubt about the relationship in the direct line or up to the second degree of the collateral line.

- *Affinity* (relationship by marriage, cann. 1092)

  Affinity, or relationship by a marriage in the direct line (for example, a man and his second wife's daughter), invalidates an attempted marriage.

- *Public Propriety* (cann. 1093)

  A marriage is invalid between a person who has established common life with another or who lives in public or notorious concubinage with a person who is of the first degree of the direct line (child or parent) of the partner (such as the daughter of the man's mistress). This impediment is known as *public propriety*.

- *Adoption* (cann. 1094)

  A marriage is invalid between an individual and another who is *related by adoption* in the direct line (parent or grandparent) or in the second degree of the collateral line (brother or sister).

2. A defect of canonical form

When Catholics marry, they are required to observe *canonical form* in celebrating the marriage rite. To observe *canonical form* means that Catholics must marry in the presence of a properly delegated priest (or deacon) and two witnesses. The official minister at the celebration (priest or deacon) must ask the couple to exchange their consent in his presence. In order for the Catholic priest or deacon to witness the marriage, at least one of the parties of the marriage must be a Roman Catholic. The cleric can witness the marriage only within his own proper territory or unless he has been delegated by the proper authority—that is, by someone with the proper power to authorize him to witness the marriage outside his parish territory. If in another parish, the cleric is to receive delegation to witness the marriage from the proper pastor of that parish where the marriage is to be celebrated.

Is it possible to get a dispensation from canonical form?

In certain circumstances it is difficult to observe *canonical form*—for example, when the non-Catholic party has a strong affiliation with his or her own faith tradition and would like their own minister to witness their marriage vows. In such a case, it may be appropriate to request a dispensation from the form used in the Catholic Church, which can normally be obtained from the bishop of the Catholic party, so that a minister of another faith tradition may witness the marriage consent on behalf of the Church. The application usually includes a request for the dispensation from the impediment for a Catholic marrying an unbaptized person or permission for the Catholic party to marry a person who is baptized into another faith tradition (see previous). Usually the local bishop is petitioned for a dispensation from form and the dispensation for a Catholic to marry an unbaptized person or permission to marry a baptized person of another faith tradition. Before granting the dispensation from form, the bishop must consult the bishop of the place where the marriage will be celebrated, if it will take place in another diocese, to make certain that there is no objection to the marriage taking place. It is also required that there be some form of public celebration of the wedding.

It is also important that if the dispensation from form has been granted and the ceremony takes place, there is only one exchange of consent, that is, that one minister receives the consent of both parties. It is not permitted for two different ministers to receive the respective consent from the two parties. A lack of form case can be examined by the tribunal through an administrative process in which proper documents that normally include a recently issued baptismal certificate of at least one of the parties, the marriage certificate that verifies that the officiant was not authorized by the Church to witness the wedding, and the civil divorce papers.

3. Defect of consent

The Catholic Church teaches that "consent makes the marriage." As a couple recites their vows in the presence of the official witnesses of the Church, they exchange consent, promising to be true to their spouse "in good times and in bad, in sickness and health," to love and honor the other "all the days of my life" (*Rite of Marriage*). It is a total giving of the one spouse to the other, with no qualifications or conditions. Once this consent is properly given, the marriage is understood to be permanent and lifelong. Regretfully, it sometimes happens that one (or both) of the parties are incapable of giving their full consent to this union or even unwilling to do so.

On what grounds could there be a defect of consent?

A defect—that is, a deficiency in the consent that was given at the time of the marriage—affects the validity of a marriage. There exists a variety of grounds that may be used by the tribunal in examining the marriage in question. Consent may be defective in the following ways:

- An *incapacity* such as *lacking the use of reason*, suffering some *grave defect of discretion of judgment*, or the *inability to assume the essential obligations of marriage* due to causes of a *psychic* nature (cann. 1095).
- *Ignorance* that marriage is a permanent union between a man and a woman, ordered to the procreation and education of children through sexual cooperation (cann. 1096).
- *Error* concerning the *person* married or an error about a *quality* of the person that was principally and directly intended (cann. 1079).
- Marriage entered *by fraud* about some quality of the other person that by its nature would seriously disturb conjugal life (cann. 1098).

- Error about the *unity*, *indissolubility*, or *sacramental dignity* of marriage that determined the will (cann. 1099).
- Simulating the marriage—giving the *external appearances* that consent was being given, while internally, by an act of the will, excluding marriage or some essential element or property of marriage (cann. 1101).
- Entering marriage on the basis of a *future condition* (cann. 1102). Marital consent placed with a past or present condition can be valid or not, depending on whether the object exists or not.
- Marriage entered into by *force* or *grave fear* from outside the person, so that marriage becomes the only viable way to be free of the fear (cann. 1103).

The tribunal will carefully review the information that has been submitted by the petitioner, contact the former respondent, and determine the proper grounds by which the marriage should be examined for possible invalidity. The petitioner and the respondent will be contacted by the court after this assessment for a notification of the grounds by which the tribunal will proceed.

Under what circumstances can the marriage bond be dissolved?

It is the teaching of the Catholic Church that a ratified (entered into by two baptized persons) and consummated (in which the partners have willingly and mutually performed the act of intercourse) marriage cannot be dissolved by any human power. There are some circumstances in which the marriage bond can be dissolved.

- *Unconsummated marriage:* A marriage entered into by two baptized persons or between a baptized person and a person who is not baptized can be dissolved by the pope for a just cause at the request of one or both parties.

- *"Pauline Privilege"*: A marriage that has been entered into by two unbaptized persons is dissolved in *favor of the faith* when a new marriage is contracted by one of the parties who receives baptism, provided the unbaptized person departs. The unbaptized person is considered to have "departed" if he or she does not wish to cohabit in peace with the baptized party or without insult to the Creator (the unbaptized party making it difficult or impossible for the Christian party to practice the faith should the unbaptized party not depart), unless after baptism the baptized person gave the other party just cause to depart. Before the baptized party can contract a new marriage, the unbaptized person is to be interviewed concerning the following:

  - Whether he or she wishes to be baptized;
  - Whether he or she wishes to cohabit in peace with the baptized party without insult to the Creator.

Since 1920 there have been cases in which dissolution of the bond was granted where one of the parties was baptized at the time of the marriage. Such a marriage is dissolved in "favor of the faith" when the party desires to become Catholic or desires to marry a Catholic. In this case, the pope dissolves the marriage in favor of the Christian faith when one of the parties of a marriage has become a Catholic or perhaps desires to marry a Catholic. This has become a more commonly used procedure.

Although the process of seeking a declaration of nullity may seem a bit daunting, please remember that the priest and pastoral staff of your parish and the personnel on the diocesan tribunal are there to help and guide you; they are not there to judge you as a person. In the next chapter, I will present information that I hope will dispel your fears as well as correct any misconceptions you may have about the process.

CHAPTER HIGHLIGHTS

- There are several ways in which a marriage may be considered invalid in the Catholic Church.
- An impediment may be present, an "obstacle" that prevents a valid celebration of a marriage, such as a man who is younger than the required age (sixteen).
- A marriage may be considered invalid if it involves a Catholic who marries without a deacon or priest officiating and no dispensation was received.
- More commonly, a marriage may be considered invalid when consent is lacking on the part of one or both of the parties.
- There are several ways, referred to as "grounds," that may be explored to determine if consent was lacking at the time the vows were exchanged.
- There are certain limited circumstances when a marriage bond may be dissolved, for example, when two unbaptized people enter into a marriage and one desires to receive baptism, the "Pauline Privilege."

4

WHY SHOULD I PETITION FOR A DECLARATION OF NULLITY?

As I said previously, people come to the Catholic Church seeking Christian Initiation or admittance into full communion with the Catholic Church with a variety of life experiences. Sometimes those desiring this initiation or admittance have been previously married and are now in a civil union. Sometimes the person is married to someone who has been previously married. It can often happen that the person who seeks admission into the Church is not able to regularize the current marriage. The Church requires that a person be free to marry prior to the celebration of the Sacraments of Initiation or full communion with the Catholic Church. For those persons who are in presumably valid marriages, no action is required before initiation (e.g., two Lutherans who are free to marry do not need to regularize their marriage when one or both are received into full communion).

I've also mentioned that very early into the inquiry, the individual and a member of a pastoral staff or team should thoroughly discuss the situation so that any needed canonical processes can be reviewed and implemented at the appropriate time. It may also be appropriate to contact the local tribunal for further information concerning the canonical procedures, such as the declaration of nullity, if questions emerge due to the possible complexity of the case.

For many individuals seeking a declaration of nullity, the prospect of reexamining a former marital union is fraught with difficulties. A partner from a former marriage may no longer have an address known to the inquirer. There may be fears that if the former spouse is contacted, it may jeopardize the present peaceful conjugal life of the petitioner. It may stir up memories of a distasteful civil divorce proceeding. There may also be fears of fees that may be difficult to pay. Perhaps most wearisome is the prospect of "dredging up" thoughts and memories from the near or distant past that one would rather not consider or bring to mind. Fortunately, for most of these scenarios, there are solutions that can bring peace of mind to the undertaking of what may at first seem onerous, legalistic, and bureaucratic.

I hope that the following information can relieve or reduce some of the fears.

CLEARING UP MISCONCEPTIONS

First, the lack of participation on the part of the former spouse does not jeopardize the annulment process.

The former spouse will be cited by the tribunal to participate (since he or she, if Catholic, has the possibility, if the marriage is declared invalid, of celebrating a marriage within the Catholic Church, should the person so desire and there be no further issues or obstacles.) Or if the former spouse is not Catholic but desires to marry a Catholic, the option of a Catholic ritual could be possible.

The tribunal is required by Church law to make every effort to contact the former spouse of the petitioner. The court will seek to obtain a thorough review of the case in question, which needs the perspective and opinions that can be provided by both parties, for the sake of justice. The tribunal, with the assistance of the petitioner, will undertake as thorough and complete a search as possible in order to notify the former spouse. However, if that spouse is not locatable after a good faith effort, the proceedings can continue in the absence of the other party.

The respondent, when contacted, will be given a specific deadline in which to respond. If the tribunal does not hear back from the respondent by that date, the case may continue, with a court officer appointed by the judge to make sure that the rights of the party absent from the process are protected.

Although a respondent may be upset when contacted by the tribunal about a pending case for a declaration of nullity of a former marriage, the tribunal attempts to provide as much information as possible about the nullity process. Very often, an education about the teachings of the Church about marriage and the annulment procedures, conveyed in a constructive and informational manner, can help alleviate any unnecessary anxiety. The respondent will also be told that he or she does not necessarily have to participate in the case if he or she does not desire to do so. At no time in the course of the proceedings will it be necessary for the petitioner to meet with the respondent; there is no "hearing" as such with both parties present. The procedure primarily involves written summaries, testimonies, and assessments submitted by the petitioner, the respondent (should he or she decide to participate), witnesses, experts, and other court personnel. Any further concerns about the required contacting of a former spouse should be addressed to the local tribunal. The tribunal is experienced in such matters and can provide good guidance.

Second, for some time a misconception has existed about the costs associated with the annulment proceeding; specifically, the notion has been perpetuated that obtaining an annulment is outrageously expensive and the decree will not be granted unless payment is forthcoming.

A question that frequently arises is whether an annulment makes the children illegitimate. The children of a marriage that has been declared invalid by the Church remain legitimate. The issue of legitimacy of children derives from civil law and is not affected by the decision of the Church's tribunal. The children remain legitimate.

GOD'S HEALING LOVE

A significant reason for pursuing the annulment is the possible therapeutic value that may come from participating in the process itself. If the inquirer has experienced a divorce, there are many possible dynamics at work. One of these is often a grieving process, as the individual deals with the "death" of a relationship. Like the various stages a person experiences when facing a terminal illness (the paradigm proposed several years ago by Dr. Elizabeth Kübler Ross, the renowned bereavement expert), so too an individual could be grappling, consciously or otherwise, with issues of which they are unaware or that refuse to be healed. In addition to the struggles of dealing with all the personal issues concomitant with a failed marriage (alimony, child support, poor self-image, and so forth), spiritual issues can arise, for example, How does God look at me after this divorce? Will I be accepted by the Church, the clergy, and the members of my church? And so forth.

Most tribunals ask the applicant to complete a questionnaire in which he or she is guided in reviewing his or her own personal history related to the marriage for which a declaration of nullity is being requested. Included in this review may be a summary of the applicant's childhood, family background, adolescence, dating experience, courtship and marriage, and history of the marriage—its difficulties and problems. Such a narrative assists the tribunal in determining possible grounds to pursue in studying the marriage in question for possible invalidity. But there can also be useful and practical effects for the petitioner: an opportunity to put perspective into the marriage—the dynamics that may have influenced what ultimately became possibly poor choices and internal dynamics in one or both parties that resulted in an incapacity or unwillingness to give full marital consent to the other person.

In examining the past marriage and some of the attendant difficulties and stresses, it is helpful to use the lens of God's faithful love. The experience of God's consoling presence and healing is particularly helpful when an applicant is undergoing a grieving process over the death of a prior relationship. Two qualities are especially necessary for this review: gentleness and patience with oneself. While the tribunal will focus primarily on the legal and technical aspects of establishing the possible invalidity of the marriage, the insightful priest or other parish minister will assist as needed and invited, with the internal, spiritual dynamics of the petitioner and any possible struggles as they undertake the procedure for an examination of their case.

CHAPTER HIGHLIGHTS

- There are many reasons why individuals apply for a declaration of nullity from a marriage tribunal.
- The Catholic Church requires that a person be free to marry or to have the present marital union considered valid prior to the celebration of the Sacraments of Initiation.
- The granting of the annulment is never conditioned on the ability to pay by the person requesting it; some dioceses have eliminated fees and many reduce any required fees based on the petitioner's ability to pay.
- Many have found the annulment experience to be healing and helpful in their personal struggles after a divorce has been obtained.

CONCLUSION

Since people come inquiring about the Roman Catholic Church from a variety of life stories and backgrounds, the RCIA process has an adaptable structure to enable it to respond better to the various life situations in which inquirers find themselves. Although the basic structure of the Rite remains constant, the time frame for participating in the rites may vary greatly. An unbaptized woman who has been married for several years to a Roman Catholic and has attended Mass with her husband and has observed and asked many questions about the Catholic faith over several years may be in a different "place" when she decides to begin the RCIA process from that of a young professional businessman who has searched from religion to religion and suddenly comes upon something attractive about the Catholic Church. Both will benefit from the RCIA but one may need more time than the other to work through the various stages with prayer, reflection, and the good guidance of the pastor, pastoral staff members, and parishioners. The ultimate end for both may be the same, but the length of time toward that end may vary significantly.

Similarly, when an inquirer approaches a local parish with a strong desire to learn about the Catholic Church and includes in their journey a marital situation that may need to be adjudicated by a marriage tribunal, extreme sensitivity is needed—not only in identifying the possible time that may be required before the reception of baptism or reception into full communion, but also, and perhaps more importantly, a sensitivity in explaining the Catholic Church's theology of marriage and the annulment process that may be needed. The careful and confidential guidance of the clergy and/or RCIA staff members in dealing with inquirers in such delicate situations cannot be overemphasized.

The RCIA process is multifaceted. It attempts to assist inquirers such as yourself as they discern how the Roman Catholic Church is the right spiritual home for them. With the assistance of a pastoral staff member and by interaction with a local faith community, you will explore a rich tradition and a vibrant sacramental theology and practice that will hopefully be the answer to questions that have been raised during your journey. It can also provide a "sacred time" for reflection upon your personal struggles, especially those related to a difficult marriage situation that may have led to divorce. Hopefully, through a guided listening process and an open heart, the pastoral staff member can gently guide you through the appropriate canonical process that may be needed to regularize a past marriage or to obtain a declaration of nullity. Once again, remember that the operative context is flexibility—there is no set time by which you are required to move forward toward the Sacraments of Initiation.

The RCIA is also an enriching experience for the parish faith community. As they walk with you and other inquirers through the various steps or stages of the process and celebrate those steps within the Sunday liturgy, normally during Lent, the community reflects with you on the paschal mystery and their own ongoing need for conversion of heart.

Once again, with each welcoming of new inquirers and the commencement of the RCIA process, the community rejoices as the discerners "hear the preaching of the mystery of Christ, the Holy Spirit opens their hearts, and they freely and knowingly seek the living God and enter the path of faith and conversion" (RCIA 1).

Although the annulment process may seem somewhat daunting, the parish staff and local tribunal will be available to assist and guide you throughout the process. We are a community of faith and believers who walk together, assisting each other in our journey of faith. May the Lord bless your journey as it continues, giving peace and encouragement as you are welcomed into the household of God!

CHAPTER HIGHLIGHTS

- Every person who decides to begin the journey toward the Roman Catholic Church comes from a unique life experience and past.
- The RCIA process involves walking with others who are discerning this journey for themselves, with Catholics who walk with the inquirers and help them throughout the process.
- Sometimes part of the journey involves a failed marital relationship that needs to be reviewed, with the possibility that a declaration of nullity may be required.

- The parish staff as well as the local marriage tribunal stands ready to assist the inquirer throughout this delicate process, which can hopefully bring about some resolution to issues of a past relationship and bring some peace of mind.

SUGGESTED READING

Coriden, James. *An Introduction to Canon Law*. Rev. ed. Mahwah, NJ: Paulist Press, 2004.

Duquin, Lorene Hanley. *Seeking an Annulment with the Help of Your Catholic Faith*. Huntington, IN: Our Sunday Visitor, 2007.

Foster, Michael Smith. *Annulment: The Wedding That Was*. Mahwah, NJ: Paulist Press, 1999.

McKenna, Kevin E. *A Concise Guide to Canon Law: A Practical Handbook for Pastoral Ministers*. Notre Dame, IN: Ave Maria Press, 2000.

Sweet, Rose. *How to Understand & Petition for Your Decree of Nullity*. Charlotte, NC: St. Benedict Press, 2012.

Vondenberger, Victoria. *Catholics, Marriages and Divorce: Real People, Real Questions*. Cincinnati, OH: St. Anthony Messenger Press, 2004.

FURTHER RESOURCES

The North American Conference of Separated and Divorced Catholics provides programs, resources, and information for the healing and recovery of those who have experienced separation or divorce. Visit their Web site at http://www.nacsdc.org/.

MY OWN NOTES

Spirit – with a broken heart – ever do anything like that? Never! Without exception, everything that a teacher has ever done to a learner because he did not understand that person would not have been done if they had been under the control of the Holy Spirit, with a broken heart.

Now turn to these verses about understanding people – Matthew 7:1-5. I believe as we look at this we find God's method. "Do not judge." Were those Pharisees judging? When I stand up here as a teacher, and I see a student back there go to sleep, how do I feel? Well, you say, "You don't understand that kid." Many times I don't. It may have been that he was sick all night. I don't begin to understand, but the reason I didn't understand that student was because there was something wrong in my heart. "Judge not, that you be not judged. For with the judgment you pronounce you will be judged, and with the measure you use it will be measured to you. Why do you see the speck that is in your brother's eye"—or why do you look at the speck that is in your student's eye—"but do not notice the log that is in your own eye? . . . first take the log out of your own eye, and then you will see clearly" (v. 3-5). When I do this I will begin to be involved with the other person.

How to Become Involved with People

Let's look again at the Lord Jesus and see the basic principles of teaching. First, the engine must be right. There must be steam in the engine, it must be on the right track and must be going itself where it wants the cars to go. Second, if the engine is going to accomplish anything and get the cars to the destination, it must be coupled to the cars. I must be intimately related to the one I am teaching. I want to emphasize again that God's method is to break up the human heart. When my heart is broken and filled with the love of God, even if I know nothing about human behavior, even if I know nothing about children, I will do that which is necessary to be involved with them.

Watch the next time you fail in your teaching. You may say, "Oh, I made a miserable mess because I didn't understand that child." Press it back to the root, and see why you did that. I challenge you to find any mistake you make in not understanding a child, and you may find there is something wrong in your own heart before the Lord.

How can I become involved with those I would teach? God desires to deliver my heart from the things which keep me from being one with people, as the Pharisee who looks at himself as right and looks down on others. I believe that the Lord himself, by the Holy Spirit, will teach that person who really seeks to follow the Lord and is determined at all costs to be like him as a teacher.

Let me ask you, do you believe that the Lord knows psychology? Some of us Christian educators in America believe that we know something that the Lord himself didn't know! Because he didn't know it when he wrote this Book, he didn't put it in this Book, so now we have to write additions to the Bible! It's ridiculous! I will say again, if a teacher is willing to pay any price, not seeking the easy way out, then the Lord by the Word of God and the Holy Spirit will reveal his way of effectively dealing with people.

Do you know what will happen if I take this approach to finding all my content and method in the Lord Jesus? Just as soon as I look at the Lord Jesus, he will tear my heart to pieces and break me down flat. Will I be trusting in myself? No! I will be trusting in the Living God. Where will I get my knowledge? From the Lord himself. Who will receive the glory? Jesus Christ. Anything accomplished? Oh, yes!

Assuming that my heart is stayed on Jehovah and is broken, and I want the Lord to take every beam out of my own eye that I might see clearly, then I will make a better teacher with this knowledge than without it.

Now may I offer some suggestions as to the kinds of things a person like this might learn? There are three areas in particular which you ought to study if you are going to understand your students.

Know the Home

The first is the home from which the student has come. Do you know what God says in the Bible that the home should be like? The home should ideally be a little model of Heaven. Just as we speak of Heaven as our heavenly home, the child's home is to be his earthly heaven. Do you know any child whose home is exactly like Heaven? Is there any wonder why that child doesn't act as he should? If you take your car and put water in the gas tank, would you expect it to run smoothly? Now you take a child that God created to live in "Heaven on earth," and put "hell on earth" in it, and see how it works. If you want to understand a particular boy, then you go back to his home – mark his home and compare it with Heaven. To the extent that the home from which this child comes is not like Heaven, he will have special needs and problems.

Know the Cultural Patterns

The second thing that is helpful in understanding children is "the way of life," or the patterns of behavior which his community imposes upon him. What is the way of life for a child born in the ghettos of the city? If a child is from a less developed part of the world, what effect does that have?

In my community everybody went to Sunday school on Sunday. Everyone spoke nicely and didn't use bad words, they were generally clean and respectable. That was the way of life. If you bring a child in and he curses, why does he do this? You say because he is a wretched sinner. Oh no! Of course he is a wretched sinner, but this is true for each of us. Why didn't you curse before you were saved? It is likely because you were brought up with a different way of life. The cultural patterns around you squeezed you into a certain mold.

Listen to Romans 12, "Be not conformed to this way of life . . . don't let it squeeze you into its mold, but be transformed by the renewing of your mind, so that you may prove what the will of God is, that which is good and acceptable and perfect" (v. 2). That's the way of life to which we are to be conformed.

A three-word description of the will of God taken from this passage is, "good, acceptable, perfect." Now let me ask you a question. Is your student's home like heaven? "Oh," you may respond, "it is more like hell on earth!" Ask yourself this. Was the effect of his or her way of life to mold them into good, acceptable and perfect? No, there is none that is good and acceptable and perfect except the One revealed in this Book.

Know the Person

The third approach that will help one understand is to look at the child himself. This can be a life-long study, but a few hints help. One of the most important things to know about this person is that they are created in God's image as one who chooses. This capacity to choose is called the "will," and the child is constantly using it. It is like a switch.

You cannot teach a person whose will is set against you. You cannot teach a child whose will is set against God. Yet how wonderful it is to instruct a child who has yielded himself to your teaching role in his life. Thus it is one of the tasks of a teacher to be as the Lord Jesus so that they can say to their students, "Take my yoke upon you, and learn from me" (Matt 11:29). In the wonderful ways of God, as the child thus yields his will to a human teacher, he is also learning to surrender himself to the Lord Jesus, the Great Teacher.

The second most important thing to understand about a child is that inside of him there is a cup or tank that must be kept full. This cup is not just for food and rest, etc., but also for such things as love and recognition and security. This is the basic root explanation of everything any child ever does. He is trying to fill that cup for himself. Yet he cannot do it. Why does he pull the little girl's hair in front of him? He is trying to get somebody to fill his cup. If you recognize him as a person, he will give himself to you. Did the Lord Jesus recognize those children they brought to him? He took them and held them in his arms. Security? If you fill the cup full, and they will come to you. We need so much of that! You must recognize that they have cups that must be filled to running over, and God demands that you fill those cups with love and recognition and security. Many children don't get this at home, so you must give it to them in appropriate ways as you teach.

The third thing to remember is that in God's order, a human being is not at birth what he or she will be at maturity. It is God's plan for each one to grow into maturity. Thus, children are constantly changing in size, in functions, and in ability in every area.

The fourth thing to understand is that children are learning constantly. "Oh," you say, "mine don't learn anything!"
Don't kid yourself! They are learning. The human being is
learning all the time. They might not be learning what you
want them to learn, but they are constantly learning, either
negatively or positively. God has made the human being
as the greatest learner in all creation, that he might be a
good disciple (learner) of Jesus Christ.

Student – Student Involvement

We have seen that the first area of training has to do with
the teacher. The Word of God says consistently that the
teacher must be right—the teacher must be this, and this,
and this if they are going to do an effective job of training.
So often the problem is in the teacher, not in the students.

The second area that we have touched on related to our
train analogy has to do with the fact that as a teacher I
must somehow be able to "hook" these students to myself. If I am going to take them somewhere, there must be
a right relationship between myself and them. If I am, as
the Lord Jesus, loving them regardless of what they do,
and if I understand the individual students, do you think
they will be closer together? What kind of teacher-student
relationships will I have? The goal is be more and more
like the Lord Jesus in the way that he interacted with his
disciples.

Let me suggest another area in which you might study.
Look with me at John 13, beginning with verse 21, where
the Lord Jesus is facing the last opportunity to teach his
disciples on earth. Let's see how he does it.

"After saying these things, Jesus was troubled in his spirit,
and testified, 'Truly, truly, I say to you, one of you will be-

tray me.'" (John 13:21). You know what happened after this, so we will skip down. "Jesus answered, 'It is he to whom I will give this morsel of bread when I have dipped it.' So when he had dipped the morsel, he gave it to Judas, the son of Simon Iscariot. Then after he had taken the morsel, Satan entered into him. Jesus said to him, 'What you are going to do, do quickly.' . . . So, after receiving the morsel of bread, he immediately went out" (v. 26-27, 30).

After Judas left, do you know what the Lord talked to them about? "When he had gone out, Jesus said, "Now is the Son of Man glorified, and God is glorified in him . . . A new commandment I give to you, that you love one another: just as I have loved you, you also are to love one another. By this all people will know that you are my disciples, if you have love for one another'" (John 13:31, 34-35).

A little while later Jesus prays for the disciples, "that they may all be one" (John 17:21). Now let me give you a broad principle. You can only teach one student at a time! Do you have 50 in your class? Well, put it down, it is still a fact that you can only teach one person at a time. Do you see what the Lord Jesus was doing in this situation? How many people did he have there before he sent Judas out? Twelve. Oh no! He had two! Now watch. It was absolutely impossible for Judas to be one with this group. The eleven were united as one, and Judas made two! When Jesus sent Judas out, how many did he have? One! You can only teach one. You know what I am talking about. Take 15 ten-year-old boys, and if they are all deciding to do what they want to do, can you effectively teach them? Not unless you get them together as one! The Lord says that to the extent that these students are all one—to that extent you are going to do a good job of teaching.

It is the teacher's responsibility to be sensitive to any problems that come up between students and by his grace and wisdom enable them to solve them. Here, in a special sense, the "peacemakers" will be blessed.

Chapter 5

The Learning Process

Each individual car of a passenger train has its own system of brakes. These are designed to be controlled from the engine, but may also be operated manually from each car. It is entirely possible that a teacher might be all that he ought to be, and the teacher-student relationship might be all that it ought to be, and the student-student relationship might be all that it ought to be, and the car will still have its brakes on! It will not budge. The teacher may love his students and they can love him, and they can have perfect understanding, and the students can all love one another, but no real learning will take place. God made people in a certain way and we learn only according to certain principles. Apart from a miracle, no one learns contrary to these basic laws of God.

I have found six principles of learning which were demonstrated in the teaching of the Lord Jesus.

Principle 1: Ability

The Lord Jesus once said to his disciples, "I still have many things to say to you, but you cannot bear them now" (John 16:12). What was he saying? "I would love to teach you more, but you are not able to learn it now." Nobody learns unless he is able to learn.

A five-year-old child is not able to learn what a ten-year-old can learn. An unsaved person who has not the Spirit of Christ cannot truly understand the things of God. Thus, there is the necessity of regeneration. A babe in Christ who has not learned to depend on the power of the Spirit cannot learn what a mature Christian can learn.

Principle 2: Material

This next point is very simple, and has been overemphasized in American teaching. In Matthew 5:1-2 we read, "Seeing the crowds, he went up on the mountain, and when he sat down, his disciples came to him. And he opened his mouth and taught them, *saying* . . ." For three long chapters following the Lord Jesus continued teaching. What did he do? *He set before them something they did not know.* Unless one is exposed to what is not known, he will never learn. The Lord's way is to show the truth in the life of the teacher and then by precept.

Principle 3: Motivation

In John 1, John the Baptist declared that Jesus was the Lamb of God. Two of his disciples left to follow Jesus. "Jesus saw them following and asked, 'What do you want?' They said . . . 'where are you staying?' 'Come,' he replied, 'and you will see'" (v. 35-39). The principle which I believe may be suggested here is that no individual learns unless for one reason or another he or she wants to. John's disciples were walking after the Lord Jesus, and he turned back to ask what they wanted. They were not sure what they were seeking, but the Lord knew. They said, "we just want to see where you live," but I believe it was much deeper than this. "What do you seek?" That to me is one of the most important principles of teaching. Unless I can make these students want to learn, they will never learn.

There are many ways of making children want to learn,

but underneath any method the principle is the same. The learning situation must in some real way touch and satisfy some basic need which the child feels. As we have seen, each child needs love, recognition, and security. The good teacher can relate the content and procedures of the lesson to the interest and needs of the student. In teaching the woman at the well, the Lord Jesus went beyond physical thirst to uncover the more intense thirst of her soul.

Principle 4: Understanding

Turn to Matthew 13 for something very clear about the teaching of the Lord Jesus. "That same day Jesus went out of the house and sat by the lake. Such large crowds gathered around him that he got into a boat and sat in it, while all the people stood on the shore. Then he told them many things in parables" (v. 1-2). Why did the Lord Jesus use parables? Paul, Peter, and Jude never used parables and yet the Lord Jesus taught using them. "The disciples came to him and asked, 'Why do you speak to the people in parables?' He replied, 'Because the knowledge of the secrets of the kingdom of heaven has been given to you, but not to them. Whoever has will be given more, and they will have an abundance. Whoever does not have, even what they have will be taken from them. This is why I speak to them in parables: Though seeing, they do not see; though hearing, they do not hear or understand'" (v. 10-13). Did they see with their physical eyes? Oh yes! But there was something beyond that. There was a willful rejection of truth, so the Lord Jesus took a truth and, for them, clothed it in a parable so that they could not play with it and trample it underfoot.

But what about the disciples? Skip down to verse 16, "But blessed are your eyes because they see, and your ears because they hear." To "hear" and to "see" means to understand. So, why did he speak in parables? The Lord Jesus took these great truths, and put them down in a story that even a child could understand. Put that down as your next basic principle of learning. Nobody learns unless he understands. In the parable of the Sower, the seed which was taken away by the birds represented truth which was taught without being understood. "Then the devil comes and takes away the word from their hearts" (Luke 8:12).

Principle 5: Participation

Let's turn to Luke 10:25. "On one occasion an expert in the law stood up to test Jesus. 'Teacher,' he asked, 'what must I do to inherit eternal life?'" Here is a man coming to the Lord Jesus. We will ignore the reason for his coming, and just look at the method that Jesus used. If somebody had come to you and said, "What must I do to be saved?" what would you do? If somebody came to you and said, "Is it wrong to smoke?" how would you answer? Most of us would just tell him what we thought he should do. But a person doesn't learn that way. Watch what Jesus does.

Jesus turned around and asked him a question, "'What is written in the Law? . . . How do you read it?' He answered, 'Love the Lord your God with all your heart . . .' 'You have answered correctly,' Jesus replied." (v. 26-28). Do you see what the Lord Jesus was doing? He got him talking. Also with Nicodemus, he asked questions and Nicodemus responded. All through his ministry the Lord Jesus would answer a question by throwing back a question, not only when the people were trying to trick him, but also when he was teaching. Do you see the basic principle? People learn only through experience, they have to be actively involved. As the Lord Jesus trained His disciples to walk by faith, he was constantly throwing them out to fend for themselves. Why? So that through experience they would learn. He knew that they wouldn't learn by just passively listening. They learned out in the ship when the storm came. A good teacher leads his or her students into experiences that cause them to learn.

Principle 6: Repetition

This final principle is very familiar. "When the disciples reached the other side, they had forgotten to bring any bread. Jesus said to them, 'Watch and beware of the leaven of the Pharisees and Sadducees.' And they began discussing it among themselves, saying, 'We brought no bread.' But Jesus, aware of this, said, 'O you of little faith, why are you discussing among yourselves the fact that you have no bread? Do you not yet perceive? Do you not remember the five loaves for the five thousand, and how many baskets you gathered? Or the seven loaves for the four thousand, and how many baskets you gathered? How is it that you fail to understand that I did not speak about bread?'" (Matt. 16:5-11).

Here is the principle I want you to see. They did not remember the lesson from their experience with the five thousand, of from the four thousand. He had to repeat the truths over and over and over again for them to get it. We learn by repetition. The Lord Jesus didn't give it to them once and expect them to learn it, he taught them over and over again.

These are the basic principles of learning. Your method must incorporate these principles, because nobody learns apart from them. These are laws of God's creation.

Conclusion

Having considered briefly some of the elements involved in the complex process of teaching, one might be tempted to respond, "Who is sufficient for these things?" The answer is two-fold.

First, no one is sufficient in themselves for this kind of teaching. To make such an admission before God is not the end of everything but rather the first step of becoming a teacher "after God's own heart."

The second answer is that only the Lord Jesus himself is sufficient for this task. Only the Lord Jesus can change a person into his own likeness. His invitation to all is "come unto me . . . and learn from me." His plan today is to teach those who come, as he did before. But now he teaches through human beings as his body.

What a privilege to be a channel through whom the Lord Jesus can teach his disciples! Shall we give ourselves afresh to the Lord Jesus that the desire of his heart might be satisfied in reaching and teaching many in these critical days?

About the Author

James M. "Buck" Hatch, served Columbia International University (CIU) as a teacher, counselor and administrator.

A pioneer in the field of biblical counseling, Hatch taught and counseled from his own experience of brokenness and pain. He grew up in an outwardly successful, but inwardly unhappy family, with his parents' marriage ending in divorce. Insecurity, timidity and brokenness marked him as a young man.

Hatch came to faith while an undergraduate student at Duke University. Feeling called into ministry, he then obtained a master of theology degree from CIU (then Columbia Bible College).

At CIU, the still-broken Hatch gained hope as Robert C. McQuilkin and others taught and modeled "a life that is supernatural, flowing from a continuous relationship with the Lord Jesus."

Mr. Hatch pastored in Mississippi for five years, then entered the University of Chicago to study anthropology, sociology and psychology. After earning a second masters degree, he joined the CIU faculty in 1947.

As a teacher, counselor, and administrator, Mr. Hatch was an integral part of Columbia International University for more than forty years. He was honored as CIU Alumni of the Year in 1998, and went to be with the Lord in 1999.

CIU

**Columbia
International
University**

*For more information about undergraduate
and graduate level teaching programs at
Columbia International University:
www.ciu.edu*

*Find out more about the Lowrie Center for
Christian Education: www.lowriecenter.com*

*For more classic resources from
Buck Hatch, visit the Buck Hatch Library:
www.buckhatchlibrary.com*

Made in the USA
Charleston, SC
26 January 2014